The Panama Canal

MIKAYA PRESS

NEW YORK

For my father, who always knows how things work, and for my mother, who loves a good story.

Special thanks to Janet G. Len-Rios, Manager
International Media and Publications
Public Relations Division Office of Executive Administration Panama Canal Commission
who tirelessly researched and answered all my questions,
and to junior editors Matthew Lehrer and Lucas Mann for their insightful comments.

BOOKS BY ELIZABETH MANN

The Brooklyn Bridge
The Great Pyramid
The Great Wall
The Roman Colosseum
The Panama Canal
Machu Picchu
Hoover Dam
Tikal
Empire State Building

Editor: Stuart Waldman
Design: Lesley Ehlers Design

Library of Congress Cataloging -in-publication Data
Mann, Elizabeth, 1948-
The Panama Canal / by Elizabeth Mann ; with illustrations by Fernando Rangel.
p.   cm.— (Wonders of the world book)
Includes index.
Summary : Relates the history of how the Panama Canal was planned
and built, including the political, international, and health
aspects of getting the project finished on time.
ISBN 1-931414-14-9
1. Panama Canal (Panama)—History—Juvenile literature.
[1. Panama Canal (Panama)— History.]   I. Rangel, Fernando, ill.
II. Title. III. Series.
F1569. C2M15 1998
972.87' 5—dc21   98-22457
                                                      CIP
                                                      AC

First paperback edition published 2006.

Printed in China

The Panama Canal

A WONDERS OF THE WORLD BOOK

BY ELIZABETH MANN
WITH ILLUSTRATIONS BY FERNANDO RANGEL

MIKAYA PRESS
NEW YORK

It was a crushing defeat, not just for Ferdinand de Lesseps, but for all of France. After nearly a decade of labor and at a cost of hundreds of millions of dollars, all that was left of the French effort to build a canal across the Isthmus of Panama was a large muddy ditch. For the hundreds of thousands of French people who had invested their money in the project, it was a disaster. Many had lost their life savings. For the families of the thousands of French and Caribbean workers who lay buried in the jungles of Panama, it was a sad tragedy.

To de Lesseps, the failure must have seemed unbelievable. After a lifetime of victories in the face of overwhelming difficulties, surely this had not happened to him. Hadn't he built the Suez Canal through the burning Egyptian desert when all the world had said "impossible"? Once he had been hailed as a hero and a genius. Now he was in disgrace, an old man afraid to leave his home. What had gone wrong?

The answer can be found on the Isthmus of Panama. Less than 50 miles wide, it is the narrowest strip of land separating the Atlantic and Pacific Oceans. The Isthmus offered a tantalizing possibility to European explorers of the 16th century. If they could somehow cross that narrow strip instead of sailing all the way around South America to reach the Pacific Ocean, they could eliminate thousands of dangerous miles from their voyages.

In 1513, Vasco Nuñez de Balboa, a Spanish explorer, led the first expedition across the Isthmus. Balboa, 190 heavily armed soldiers, and several native guides struggled through some of the most dense and mountainous rain forest in the world. It took them a month to travel 50 miles, but they made it to the Pacific. Ever since then, Europeans and Americans have tried to find easier ways to cross Panama.

Not long after Balboa's expedition, the Spanish built a road through the jungle. They called it the *Camino Real* (Royal Road), but it was really a muddy mule trail. They used it to transport gold that they had stolen from the Inca people of Peru. The gold was carried by ship from Peru to the Pacific end of the *Camino Real*. There it was loaded onto mules for the trip through the jungle to the Atlantic end of the trail, where other ships waited to carry it back to Spain.

Traveling across the Isthmus would not only be shorter, it would be safer than sailing through the notoriously rough seas at the tip of South America.

Many years later, in 1855, American businessmen built a single-track railroad across Panama. A one-way ticket cost $25. It was an exorbitant amount of money at that time, but prospectors racing to California to make their fortunes during the Gold Rush were happy to pay it. It was faster to take a ship to Panama, ride the railroad across the Isthmus to the Pacific, and take a second ship to California than it was to travel overland across the United States.

Whether it was a trail or a railroad that was being built, the thick jungle, mountainous terrain, torrential rainfall, and deep, slick mud made life miserable and hazardous for those unfortunate enough to be working in Panama. Poisonous snakes, alligators, and jaguars added to their troubles. Of all the problems the workers faced, the deadliest was disease. Untold numbers died while building the *Camino Real,* and at least 6,000 more were buried alongside the Panama Railroad.

Panama was as lovely as it was dangerous. Travelers were dazzled by the beauty of the rain forest, with its lush trees and vines, colorful flowers, and exotic birds and animals.

Ferdinand de Lesseps faced the same problems when he began planning his canal across Panama. He used his experience building the Suez Canal in Egypt to guide him. There he had dug for 105 miles through the Egyptian desert to connect the Mediterranean Sea with the Red Sea. As difficult as that task had been, the problems he had faced there had not prepared him for conditions in Panama. And he hadn't learned from the experiences of either the Spanish or the Americans who had tackled the Isthmus before him. As a result, de Lesseps underestimated his two greatest opponents: disease and the mountainous jungle. Battling them led to bankruptcy and failure.

Although the French canal project died, the idea of a canal remained very much alive, particularly in the mind of an American named Theodore Roosevelt.

Roosevelt believed that the United States needed a strong navy. A strong navy was one whose battleships could effectively patrol all the world's oceans. A canal across Panama would make it easier for American battleships to move between oceans, and that would make the navy stronger. When Roosevelt became President in 1901, he devoted himself to building the canal.

When the French stopped working in Panama in 1889,
they left behind many steam shovels and other machines.
Abandoned equipment was quickly swallowed by the jungle,
as were the graves of thousands of workers.

At that time, Panama belonged to a larger country, Colombia. Panama was a "department," a part of Colombia, just as a state is a part of the United States. Roosevelt wanted the government of Colombia to sign a treaty allowing the United States to build a canal through the Department of Panama. The Colombians thought the treaty was unfair and refused to sign it. Roosevelt was impatient, too impatient to spend time negotiating with the Colombian government. He thought it would be easier to get the treaty he wanted if he only had to deal with the people of Panama.

Not all Panamanians were happy being part of Colombia. Many wanted independence. In 1903, Roosevelt quietly sided with these revolutionaries. He sent two American gunboats to Panama to lend American support to a rebellion against Colombia. When the revolution, which lasted all of 3 days, was over, the Department of Panama had become an independent nation, the Republic of Panama. Just 12 days later, a treaty was signed between the U.S. and Panama.

Unfortunately for the new nation, the hastily signed treaty was worse for Panama than the one that the Colombians had rejected. The Americans were given permission to build a canal. They were given an enormous territory, called the Canal Zone, in which to build it. They were given tremendous authority in the rest of Panama. In return, the Panamanians were given less money than they would have received under the Colombia treaty and a promise that the U.S . would protect Panama's independence.

By helping the Panamanians to rebel against Colombia, Roosevelt had committed an illegal act. He had violated an existing treaty (the one that had allowed the Panama Railroad to be built) in which the U.S. had promised to protect Colombia's interests. At first, many people were outraged. There was a worldwide outcry against the treaty violation, but it soon faded. Newspapers stopped writing articles about the American interference in Panama and angry arguments in the American government about the president's action died out. Congress eventually voted to support what Roosevelt had done.

400 U.S. Marines came ashore from the gunboats. They were a threatening sight to the Colombian soldiers who were assigned to defend the Department of Panama. The Columbians surrendered without a shot being fired.

Roosevelt charged ahead with the canal, determined to succeed where de Lesseps had failed. The American engineers he sent to Panama faced the same enormous difficulties that the French engineers had faced in 1881, but there was one important difference. The French had been financed by a private company, which had run out of money. The Americans were backed by the unlimited wealth and resources of the United States government. Bankruptcy, at least, would not be a problem.

Disease continued to be a problem, one that was much harder to solve. Nearly 20,000 workers had died during the French canal construction. Yellow fever and malaria had been dangerous killers then, and they continued to kill when the Americans took over. Roosevelt realized that the canal would never be built if workers were sick and dying. He sent a world-famous expert on tropical disease, Dr. William Gorgas, to Panama to lead the fight against yellow fever and malaria.

Dr. Gorgas had earned his reputation by completely wiping out yellow fever on the island of Cuba in less than a year. He had done it by getting rid of the mosquitoes that spread the disease. It was a new and unusual approach, but it had worked.

Despite the success in Cuba, many people refused to accept the idea that mosquitoes spread disease. They clung to an old belief that yellow fever, malaria, and other diseases were caused by the damp night air of the tropics. Because of this, Dr. Gorgas received very little cooperation in his effort to control mosquitoes in Panama, and disease continued to claim lives.

Dr. Gorgas isolated yellow fever patients in screened enclosures to keep mosquitoes from biting them and spreading the disease to others.

Workers had orders to empty or cover all water containers so they wouldn't become nurseries for future generations of deadly mosquitoes.

In 1905, an outbreak of yellow fever caused a terrible panic in the Canal Zone. People fled the country and canal construction came to a standstill. Only then did Gorgas receive the supplies and workers he needed to launch a thorough campaign against the disease-bearing insects.

Yellow fever is spread by a single type of mosquito, *Stegomyia fasciata*. The mosquitoes spread the yellow fever virus by biting a sick person and then biting and infecting healthy people. *Stegomyia* is the only kind of mosquito that can transmit the yellow fever virus, and there is no other way for the disease to spread. When the mosquito is eliminated, the disease disappears.

Fortunately for Dr. Gorgas, *Stegomyia* mosquitoes are very fussy about certain things. The females will only lay their eggs in clean, fresh water. Since water like this was most likely to be found near people's homes, that was where the mosquitoes could be found. With this knowledge, and with the 4,000 workers now assigned to his Sanitary Department, Gorgas was able to focus an effective attack against the tiny, deadly enemy.

To prevent new mosquitoes from being hatched, Sanitary Department workers got rid of water where eggs could be laid. To keep the insects away from people, they sprayed buildings with insecticide and put screens in all the windows. It was a tremendous effort, but it paid off. In 18 months, Dr. Gorgas completely eliminated yellow fever in Panama.

Battling malaria was more difficult. Malaria is spread by a different kind of mosquito, *Anopheles albimanus.* Unlike the *Stegomyia*, the *Anopheles* females don't care where they lay their eggs. Any standing water, no matter how dirty, can serve as a breeding ground. That means that they can live anywhere, not just near people's homes, so they were harder to locate than *Stegomyia.* And in a rainy country like Panama, it's impossible to eliminate every muddy puddle. *Anopheles* mosquitoes continued to breed and malaria continued to claim victims, but the massive effort was not wasted. Between 1906 and 1914 Dr. Gorgas reduced the number of malaria cases by 90%.

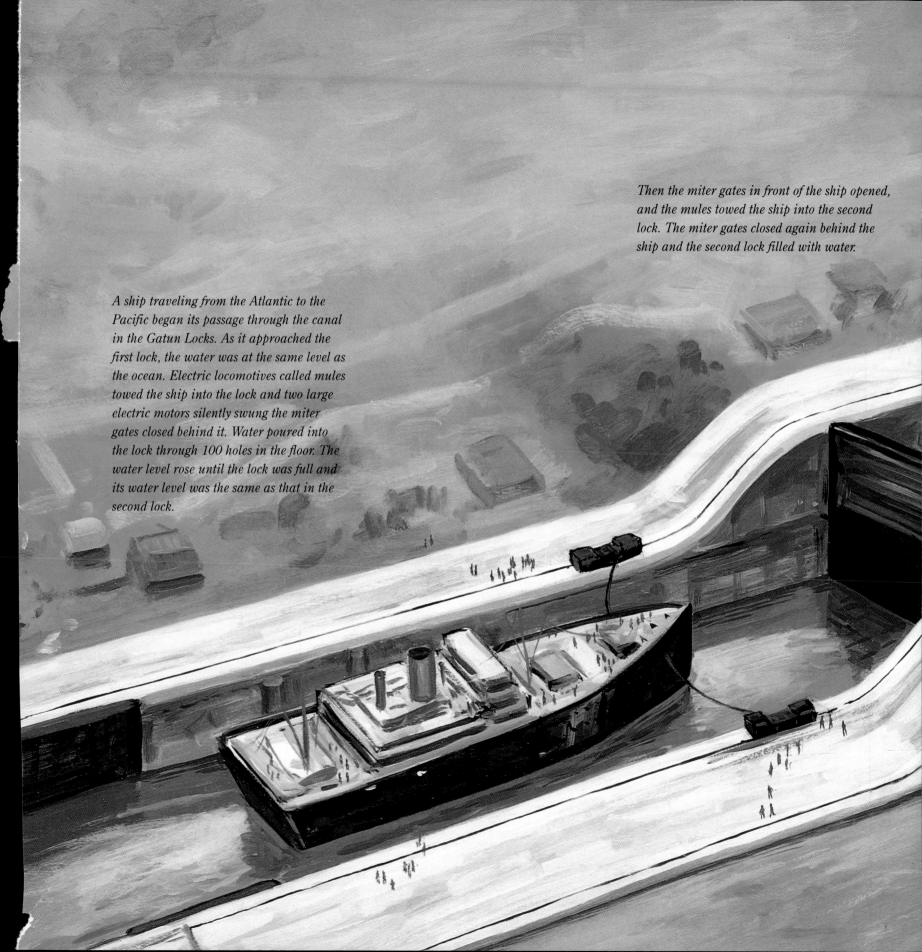

Then the miter gates in front of the ship opened, and the mules towed the ship into the second lock. The miter gates closed again behind the ship and the second lock filled with water.

A ship traveling from the Atlantic to the Pacific began its passage through the canal in the Gatun Locks. As it approached the first lock, the water was at the same level as the ocean. Electric locomotives called mules towed the ship into the lock and two large electric motors silently swung the miter gates closed behind it. Water poured into the lock through 100 holes in the floor. The water level rose until the lock was full and its water level was the same as that in the second lock.

The Americans faced another tremendous problem in Panama. They were building according to the French plan, which called for a canal whose waterway was at sea level from end to end. De Lesseps had always pictured a glistening, uninterrupted path of water across Panama, just like the Suez Canal. He refused to believe that digging down to sea level through Panama's forbidding mountains would be a far more difficult job than digging through the flat sand of the Egyptian desert.

A few French engineers had criticized the sea level plan, pointing out that it would take decades to excavate such huge, unimaginable amounts of earth and rock. De Lesseps had ignored the warnings and gone ahead with the sea level plan. The money and effort wasted pursuing this unrealistic idea had contributed as much to the French failure in Panama as disease had.

Whether they were French or American, engineers were astonished by the overwhelming difficulty of working in the jungle.

A lock canal, though it meant less digging, was a far more complicated work of engineering than a sea level canal. Stevens fought for permission to begin the lock canal plan, but it was up to George Goethals, who took over as Chief Engineer in 1907, to complete it. For the next 7 years, he tirelessly supervised every detail of the gargantuan construction project.

Locks had been used to raise and lower ships for centuries, but the ones that Goethals built in Panama were truly unique. They were larger and more sophisticated than any on earth. They were the first ever to be powered by electricity (a remarkable feat at a time when many American homes and factories did not have electricity). And never before had such large structures been built entirely of concrete.

In all, there were 12 locks, 6 at each end of the canal. They were arranged in pairs, so that ships could move through the canal in two directions at once. Each pair was formed by 3 massive concrete walls. Each lock was 1,000 feet long, 110 feet wide and 70 to 80 feet deep. Enormous hollow steel gates, called miter gates, closed the ends of each lock.

To get a sense of the size of a Panama lock, imagine standing at the bottom of one end of a lock. The concrete walls on either side of you are as tall as a 7-story building. The miter gates at the far end of the lock are nearly 4 city blocks away!

Atlantic Ocean

A sea level canal was not the only option. Another kind of canal, a lock canal, was a possibility that made more sense on the Isthmus. In a lock canal, the waterway climbs up and over the land. It doesn't have to be dug all the way down to sea level. Much less excavation is required, a tremendous advantage.

The Americans knew about the disastrous results when the French had tried to build at sea level. Still, the notion of a flat, smooth waterway, like the canal at Suez, must have been powerfully appealing. Just as de Lesseps had ignored the experience of the Americans who built the Panama Railroad, so Roosevelt chose to ignore the French experience in Panama. Despite strong indications that it wasn't such a good idea, he sent the first Americans to Panama in July of 1904 with orders to build a sea level canal.

By December of 1905, John Stevens, Chief Engineer of the Panama Canal, had become convinced that a sea level canal could never be built. His first-hand experience of the conditions in Panama had shown him that it was impossible, but he did not have the authority to change the plan. Only President Roosevelt and the United States Congress could do that. Stevens made three trips to Washington, D. C., and at last persuaded them that only a lock canal could succeed in Panama.

The canal builders had yet another large and dangerous obstacle to overcome: the Chagres River.

The Chagres was the largest river in Panama. It began deep in the rain forest and twisted and turned for 120 miles until it spilled out into the Atlantic. When it was swollen by tropical rains, it became turbulent and unpredictable. During a heavy rainfall it could rise more than 20 feet in a single day, flooding everything in its path. It had destroyed many Panamanian villages. It would certainly be able to destroy a canal.

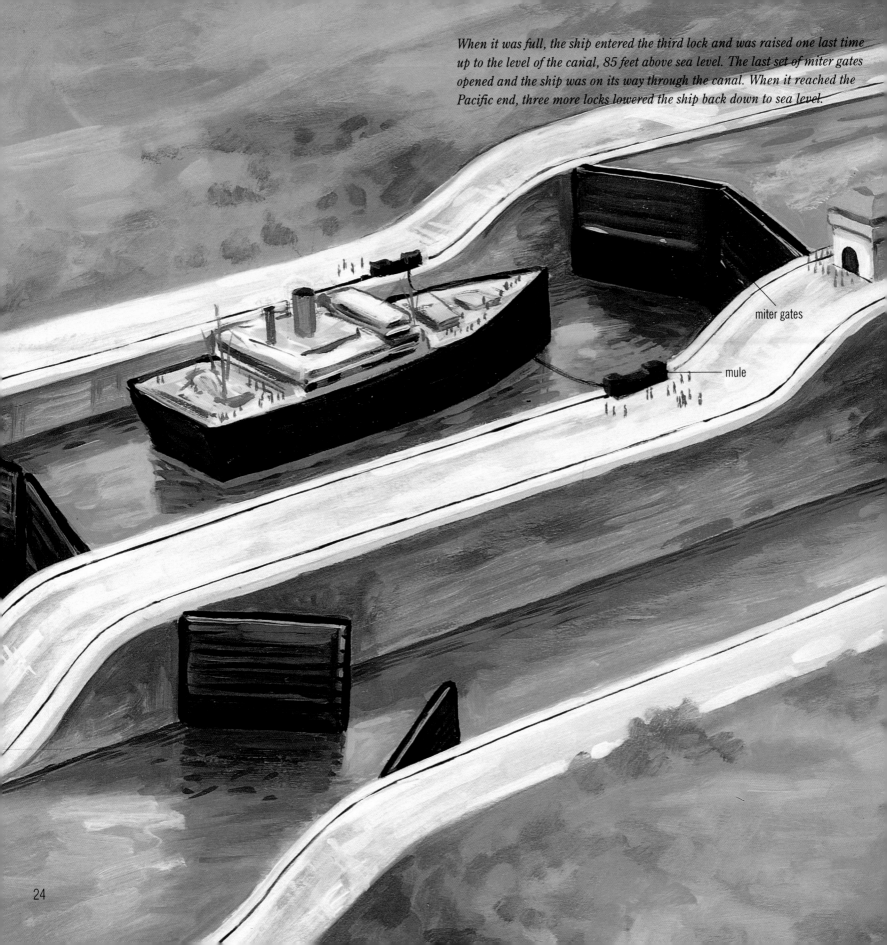

When it was full, the ship entered the third lock and was raised one last time up to the level of the canal, 85 feet above sea level. The last set of miter gates opened and the ship was on its way through the canal. When it reached the Pacific end, three more locks lowered the ship back down to sea level.

miter gates

mule

24

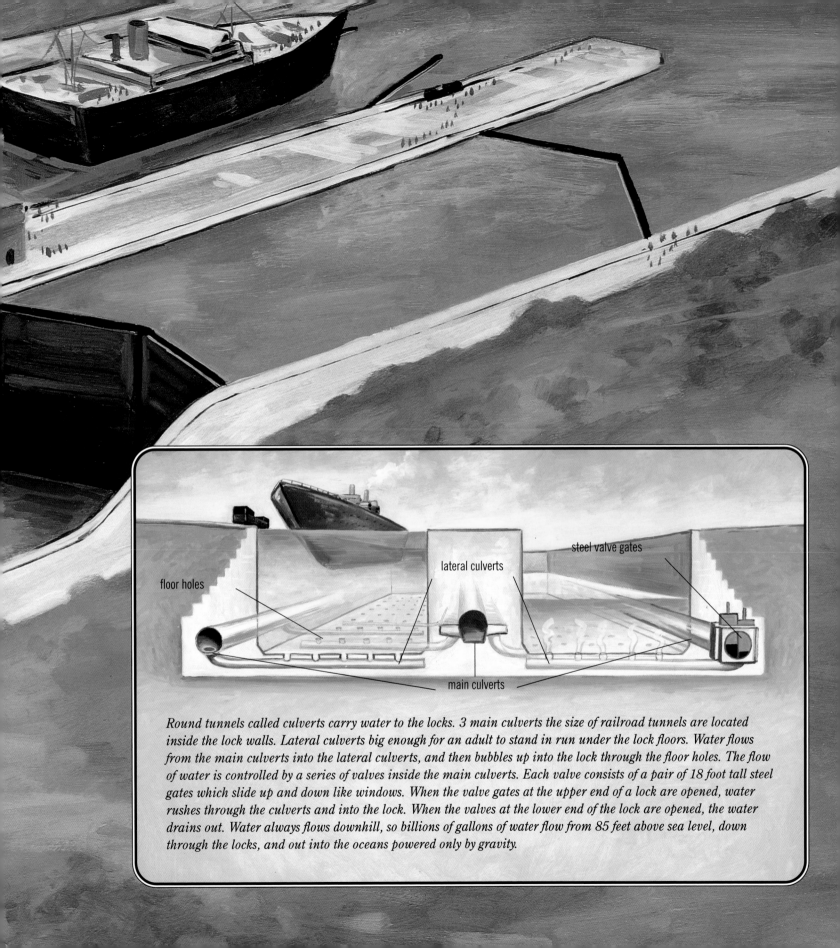

floor holes

lateral culverts

steel valve gates

main culverts

Round tunnels called culverts carry water to the locks. 3 main culverts the size of railroad tunnels are located inside the lock walls. Lateral culverts big enough for an adult to stand in run under the lock floors. Water flows from the main culverts into the lateral culverts, and then bubbles up into the lock through the floor holes. The flow of water is controlled by a series of valves inside the main culverts. Each valve consists of a pair of 18 foot tall steel gates which slide up and down like windows. When the valve gates at the upper end of a lock are opened, water rushes through the culverts and into the lock. When the valves at the lower end of the lock are opened, the water drains out. Water always flows downhill, so billions of gallons of water flow from 85 feet above sea level, down through the locks, and out into the oceans powered only by gravity.

A lock raises and lowers ships in much the same way that an escalator raises and lowers people. When you ride an escalator, you step onto a step and it rises, carrying you up with it. When a ship enters a lock, gates at both ends of the lock chamber are closed and water fills the lock. As the water level rises, it carries the ship up to the next level. In this old drawing of a 17th century lock, the ship has already entered the lock L through the gates C. The gates have closed behind it, the lock has filled with water, and the gates A have opened in front of it. Now the ship is about to leave the first lock and proceed through the channel D to the next lock, where it will be raised again.

The lock canal plan solved the Chagres problem. It called for a dam to be built across the river just before it emptied into the Atlantic. The river would back up behind the dam, creating Gatun Lake. The Chagres would still rise during the rainy season, but instead of overflowing its banks and destroying the countryside, its waters would be harmlessly absorbed into the enormous lake.

In addition to taming the wild and destructive river, the lake would actually become a part of the canal. Nearly half of a ship's 50 mile trip through the canal would be made on the tranquil waters of Gatun Lake, 85 feet above sea level. The part of the canal created by the lake required no excavation, a tremendous saving of time and money.

Gatun Dam was the largest in the world to be built of earth. It was $1 \frac{1}{2}$ miles long and $\frac{1}{2}$ mile wide at the bottom. As the river backed up and began to fill in the low-lying areas behind the dam, 164 square miles of rain forest slowly disappeared. The rising water swallowed villages, cemeteries, several miles of the original French canal, and a big section of the Panama Railroad. Thousands of Panamanians were forced to move from their homes. At the end of 4 years, only the tops of the highest hills could still be seen. They had become islands in the world's largest artificial lake.

52 million gallons of water are used in the locks every time a ship passes through the canal. Billions and billions of gallons are needed every year. Gatun Lake is a gigantic storage tank, guaranteeing a steady supply of water for the locks, even in the dry season. Thanks to the torrential jungle rains, the lake is endlessly refilled.

The Chagres River before it was dammed.

Once the dam was built, the Chagres slowly filled in the valleys and lowlands, creating Gatun Lake.

Dead trees and hilltops protrude through the lake's calm surface.

The formidable Cordillera Mountains presented another great challenge to the builders. Thanks to the lock canal plan, the channel through the Cordilleras didn't have to be excavated all the way down to sea level, but there was still a tremendous amount of digging to be done. Culebra Cut, as this section was called, was only 9 miles long, but it turned out to be the most difficult, dangerous, and heartbreaking part of the job.

An astonishing amount of earth and rock, called spoil, was dug from Culebra Cut and hauled away. Some excavation was done by hand with picks and shovels, but most was done with dynamite and heavy machinery. Powerful air drills bored holes in the rock for dynamite charges. Gigantic coal-burning steam shovels clawed tons of spoil from the hillsides and loaded it onto dirt trains. Railroad tracks lined the sides of Culebra Cut, and dozens of dirt trains raced back and forth from morning til night carrying spoil out of the Cut. Some spoil was used to build Gatun Dam, and some was taken to other dumping areas.

Workers had to dig down 272 feet through the highest rocky ridge, creating a channel that was as deep as a 25-story building is tall. Culebra Cut was so unbelievably enormous that thousands of tourists traveled to Panama every year to see it with their own eyes.

Mudslides were a serious problem in Culebra Cut, and they worsened as the channel grew deeper. The sides of the channel were very steep. When the ground became saturated and heavy during the 8 - month rainy season, the sides would collapse and slide downhill. Acres of mud and rock moved like glaciers, burying gigantic locomotives and steam shovels, tearing up railroad tracks, and filling in the bottom of the Cut. A slide could destroy months of excavation in a single day.

The slides were maddening for the work crews. As they excavated, the channel became deeper, and its sides became steeper. Steeper sides caused more slides, which meant even more digging. The only way to prevent slides was to make the sides less steep by widening the cut. Doing that, of course, required even more excavation. It seemed to many workers that the digging would never end.

Thousands of men worked all day long under the punishing tropical sun. By noontime the temperature was over 100°, sometimes reaching 130°. Daily rain showers were short, but drenching. When they ended, the air was just as hot, and even more humid, and the work site was a slippery, treacherous sea of mud. The constant, harsh racket from the trains, drills, and steam shovels was earsplitting. The air was blackened by the coal smoke that poured from the locomotives and steam shovels.

After the workers left for the day, dynamite charges were exploded. Then fresh crews arrived and worked all night refueling and repairing the machinery, moving railroad tracks, and preparing for the next day's work.

Day or night, accidents were a constant worry. Dynamite was especially hazardous. Sometimes charges exploded unexpectedly when struck by lightning, or by a steam shovel scoop, or sometimes for no reason at all. Many workers died or lost arms and legs in terrible accidents.

American workers lived in airy, spacious homes with screened windows, and relaxed in comfortable clubrooms. Their children attended well-run schools.

For some workers, the living conditions provided for them in Panama made up for the risks and discomforts of the working conditions. Many Americans would remember their years in the Canal Zone as the finest of their lives. They were given comfortable housing, and medical care was free. Salaries were higher than at home, and good food and clothing were inexpensive. There were schools, churches, social clubs, and plenty of baseball games. More than anything, the Americans who stayed in the Canal Zone developed a fierce pride in their work and in being part of a project of worldwide importance. It was a story they would tell their grandchildren.

From the unscreened windows in their homes to the overcrowded schools attended by their children, living conditions in Panama were worse for the Caribbean workers. It was the official American policy in the Canal Zone to keep black workers segregated from white workers.

Other workers, especially those who came from the Caribbean Islands of Barbados and Jamaica, would not cherish such fond memories. The Caribbeans, the majority of the workforce, were black. Though many of them shared the feelings of pride at being a part of a historic effort, they did not share in the benefits. They were paid less than the lowest paid white worker and, no matter what their skills, they had no hope of being promoted. They lived in shacks in the jungle or in crowded slums. Black Caribbeans suffered a higher rate of death from accidents and disease than any other group in the Canal Zone.

Despite the delays caused by the Culebra Cut mudslides, work on the canal was completed 6 months ahead of schedule, due largely to Goethals' careful management.

On August 15, 1914 an old cement boat, the S.S. *Ancon,* decorated with bright flags, made the first official passage through the Panama Canal. The trip was smooth, the locks worked perfectly. It was an event worthy of great celebration, but there were no festivities. Instead, the day on which the Atlantic and Pacific Oceans were joined, a day which had been awaited for decades, came and went with barely a mention in the world's newspapers.

World War I had been declared on August 3. Nothing else seemed important.

The canal was a costly undertaking in every way. The American government spent $352 million in Panama, an unheard of amount of money at that time. The cost in terms of human suffering was much more disturbing: 5,609 people died during the American construction. Add to that the estimated deaths during the French canal construction, and the total reaches a horrifying 25,000.

And yet, the Panama Canal stands as one of the greatest accomplishments of the 20th century. It's a masterpiece of engineering, one that works as smoothly today as it did in 1914. That it was built at all is impressive. That it was built in spite of the difficult terrain and brutal climate of Panama is absolutely astounding.

Stevens, Gorgas, and Goethals are the best known heroes of the canal, but they were not the only ones. Between 1904 and 1914, tens of thousands of people from 68 different countries worked in Panama. Their ingenuity, courage, sacrifice, and hard, hard work were every bit as important to the canal as its engineering. It was their extraordinary effort that built the Panama Canal.

Workers from India.

Caribbean workers arriving by boat from Barbados.

Spanish workers.

American engineers.

JOHN STEVENS CHIEF ENGINEER 1905·1907

Atlantic Ocean

Gatun Locks

Gatun Dam

Gatun Lake

DR. WILLIAM C. GORGAS CHIEF SANITARY OFFICER 1904·1914

Chagres River

Canal Zone Boundary

Culebra Cut

Panama Railroad

Pedro Miguel Locks

Miraflores Locks

Canal Zone Boundary

THEODORE ROOSEVELT U.S. PRESIDENT
1901•1908

GEORGE GOETHALS CHIEF ENGINEER
1907•1914

The Panama Canal never provided the important military advantage that Roosevelt had anticipated, but the benefits to commercial shipping have been tremendous. Nearly 750,000 ships of every size and kind from every country in the world have passed through it, with incalculable savings of time and money. The Panama Canal has made the world smaller and shortened the distances between people and nations.

The United States has maintained and operated the canal since 1914, but that will soon change. Panamanians had long resented that the treaty signed in 1903 gave the American government so much power in Panama. They believed that they were unfairly taken advantage of by a larger and more powerful nation. Over the years there were demonstrations, and sometimes violent riots, protesting the American presence in Panama. Gradually, the American government came to see the Panamanian point of view. In 1977, a new treaty was negotiated between the United States and Panama. According to the new treaty, the U.S. will officially turn the Panama Canal and the Canal Zone over to Panama on December 31, 1999.

FACTS

length of canal— 50 miles

length of Culebra Cut — 9 miles

length of canal on Gatun Lake— 24 miles

area of Gatun Lake— 164 square miles

elevation of Gatun Lake— 85 feet above sea level

amount of water used by one ship going through canal— 52 million gallons

total number of locks— 12

length of each lock— 1000 feet

width of each lock— 110 feet

depth of locks— 70-80 feet

minimum depth of water in canal— 45 feet

rise in elevation of ship going through canal— 85 feet

French construction— 1881-1889

American construction—1904-1914

INDEX

CREDITS

Panama Canal Commission, Courtesy of the National Archives: *pp.16-17, 36, 38, 43-45*
Panama Canal Commission, Courtesy of the Library of Congress: *p. 43 (middle right)*
Courtesy of the National Archives: *p. 45 (top right)*
Fernando Rangel: *pp: 5, 9, 10, 13, 14, 18, 22-25, 27, 29, 30-31, 32, 35, 41, 44-45*